PIANO • VOCAL • GUITAR

THE SONGS OF BURTON LANE

ISBN 0-7935-0085-0

Hal Leonard Publishing Corporation
7777 West Bluemound Road P.O. Box 13819 Milwaukee, WI 53213

BURTON LANE
COMPOSER

Burton Lane has managed throughout a long and successful career as a popular composer, to remain, at the same time, an artist's artist. From the very beginning of his professional life in 1927 when he signed with the Remick Music Company, becoming Tin Pan Alley's youngest songwriter at age 15, Lane has had the affection, as well as the respect, of his fellow songwriters.

When he was 17, he met and played some of his melodies for George and Ira Gershwin. George was tremendously impressed and gave Lane great encouragement. At the same time, Ira introduced Lane to E.Y. (Yip) Harburg. Many years later, Lane and Harburg were to write the great score for the stage hit FINIAN'S RAINBOW.

During the next few years, Lane wrote music for four musical revues, all played on Broadway simultaneously. Collaborating with Howard Dietz, he wrote two songs for THREE'S A CROWD. With Harold Adamson, he wrote one song for THE THIRD LITTLE SHOW, two songs for SINGIN' THE BLUES and almost the entire score for the ninth edition of Earl Carroll's VANITIES.

In 1933 the Irving Berlin Publishing Company sent Lane and Harold Adamson to California on a six week trial contract to see if they could place some of their songs in motion pictures. Lane's first screen credits were three songs he had written with Adamson. The picture was M-G-M's DANCING LADY, starring Joan Crawford and Clark Gable and the hit song of that film was EVERYTHING I HAVE IS YOURS. That song, written 56 years ago, is still an active standard in the ASCAP repertoire.

Something happened in 1934 that Lane is most proud of, although he never received credit for it. He discovered a young child singer who was then 11 years old. He brought her to the attention of the M-G-M executives. He played for her audition and they signed her. Her name was Frances Gumm, and this young child became one of the studio's greatest stars. You know her by the name of Judy Garland.

For the next 22 years, Lane became one of the movies top songwriters, writing music for over 30 films, as well as the musical scores for a number of Broadway shows.

Broadway interrupted his coast career in 1939 when Lane, working with E.Y. Harburg, composed the musical score for the hit show HOLD ON TO YOUR HATS, the last show in which the great Al Jolson was to appear.

Then back to Hollywood where Lane received his first Academy Award nomination in 1941 for HOW ABOUT YOU, the hit song from M-G-M's BABES ON BROADWAY, which starred Mickey Rooney and Judy Garland, the young child Lane had discovered. The lyrics were written by Ralph Freed.

In 1944 Lane started to write the musical score for the Olson and Johnson Broadway revue LAFFING ROOM ONLY. The great Al Dubin was to write the lyrics, but Dubin became ill and passed away leaving Lane to supply lyrics to his own melodies. The song FEUDIN' AND FIGHTIN' emerged as the hit song of that show.

In 1946 Lane and Harburg wrote FINIAN'S RAINBOW. Lane has said that in working on this show, because he had such respect for the libretto, he was more concerned with writing music of quality than in trying to write commercial songs. And yet, eight songs out of a score of eleven became big standard hits. HOW ARE THINGS IN GLOCCA MORRA and OLD DEVIL MOON are examples of the quality Lane achieved in this score.

The movies beckoned again, this time with Lane and Alan Jay Lerner providing songs for ROYAL WEDDING starring Fred Astaire and Jane Powell. This film won him his second "Oscar" nomination as the composer of the hit song TOO LATE NOW. In 1955 Lane decided to move back to New York so that he could concentrate more on writing Broadway shows, his first love.

In 1957 Lane was elected President of the American Guild of Authors and Composers, now known as The Songwriters Guild of America. He remained in that post for ten terms. In 1966 the Guild, in appreciation for what Lane had done for his fellow songwriters, awarded him the first Sigmund Romberg Award. This is an honor he finds most gratifying because it was given him by his peers.

In 1963 he and Alan Jay Lerner teamed once again. ON A CLEAR DAY YOU CAN SEE FOREVER won him the "Grammy" Award for his score on the original cast album plus raves from the critics.

In 1971 he was voted into the Songwriters Hall of Fame. He is now in his third term as an ASCAP board member. Thus Burton Lane, the popular artist's artist, will never lack for the love of his public or of his peers.

COMPOSER

Walter Kerr

reviewing FINIAN'S RAINBOW in New York Times 1967:

"I'll confine myself to three wishes. First wish: that composer Burton Lane would compose, oh, 40 or 50 more scores for the tone-deaf musical comedy stage. (Nothing unreasonable in that one.) If Burton Lane won't compose as often as his conscience should compel him to, then all other musicals should slip 'IF THIS ISN'T LOVE' into their own scores just so we won't spend our evenings yearning for it."

Howard Taubman

reviewing ON A CLEAR DAY in New York Times 1965:

"The songs have bright charming lyrics by Mr. Lerner and a sheaf of new tunes by Mr. Lane that have more melodic grace and inventive distinction than has been heard in years."

John S. Wilson

reviewing ON A CLEAR DAY cast album in New York Times 1965:

"Lane has composed his score with a feeling for the real heartbeat of the popular musical theatre. This is neither pseudo-opera nor background for recitative. It is the melodic, rhythmic, memorable kind of music that was once practically the total reason for the existence of musical comedy."

T H E   S O N G S   O F
BURTON LANE
(BY SHOW)

THE SONGS OF
BURTON LANE
(BY TITLE)

EVERYTHING I HAVE IS YOURS

Lyrics by HAROLD ADAMSON
Music by BURTON LANE

Chorus *(slow with expression)*

Eve-ry-thing I Have Is Yours, You're part of me____

Eve-ry-thing I Have Is Yours my des-ti-ny____

I would glad-ly give the sun to you If the sun were on-ly mine

I would glad-ly give the earth to you and the stars that shine.

Adolph Zukor
presents

COLLEGE SWING

GEORGE BURNS
and GRACIE ALLEN
MARTHA RAYE
BOB HOPE

Edward E. Horton
Ben Blue
Betty Grable
Jackie Coogan
Florence George
John Payne
Skinnay Ennis
Directed by RAOUL WALSH
A PARAMOUNT PICTURE

MOMENTS LIKE THIS

Lyrics by FRANK LOESSER
Music by BURTON LANE

HOW'DJA LIKE TO LOVE ME

Lyrics by FRANK LOESSER
Music by BURTON LANE

Moderato (*Rhythmically*)

Voice

You're just a quick ro-manc - er___ You're just a fly-by-night___

But I'm a take-a-chanc - er,___ So come on and hold me tight___

17

THE LADY'S IN LOVE WITH YOU

Lyric by FRANK LOESSER
Music by BURTON LANE

I HEAR MUSIC

Lyrics by FRANK LOESSER
Music by BURTON LANE

Refrain

DANCING ON A DIME

Lyrics by FRANK LOESSER
Music By BURTON LANE

Now I'd nev-er dream of mak-ing love with so man-y peo-ple near. No, I'd nev-er dream of mak-ing love, but love is here.

YOU'RE ALL THE WORLD TO ME

Lyrics by ALAN JAY LERNER
Music by BURTON LANE

Chorus Lively Fox Trot

You're like Pa-ris in A-pril and May___
You're Lake Co-mo when dawn is a-glow___

You're New York on a sil-ver-y day___
You're Sun Val-ley right af-ter a snow___

A Swiss Alp as the sun grows faint-er; You're Loch
A mu-se-um, a Per-sian pa-lace, You're my

Lo-mond when Au-tumn is the paint-er.
shin-ing Au-ro-ra Bo-re-a-lis.

You're moon-light on a
You're like Christ-mas at

TOO LATE NOW

Lyric by ALAN JAY LERNER
Music by BURTON LANE

HOW COULD YOU BELIEVE ME WHEN I SAID I LOVE YOU WHEN YOU KNOW I'VE BEEN A LIAR ALL MY LIFE?

Lyric by ALAN JAY LERNER
Music By BURTON LANE

PATTER

Blues tempo (in four)

said you would love me long, ___ and nev-er would do me wrong. ___

And faith-ful you'd al - ways be, ___ (Boy) oh,

ba-by, you must be loon-y to trust a low-er than low two-tim-er like me. ___

(Girl) You said I'd have ev-'ry-thing, a beau-ti-ful dia-mond ring, a bun-ga-low by the sea. (Boy) You're real-ly na-ive to ev-er be-lieve a full of ba-lo-ney phon-ey like me. (Girl) Say!

HOW ABOUT YOU

Lyric by RALPH FREED
Music by BURTON LANE

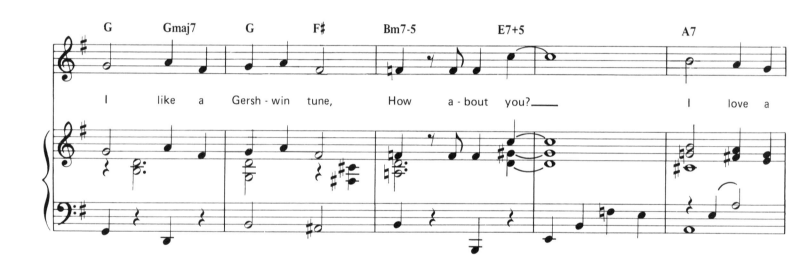

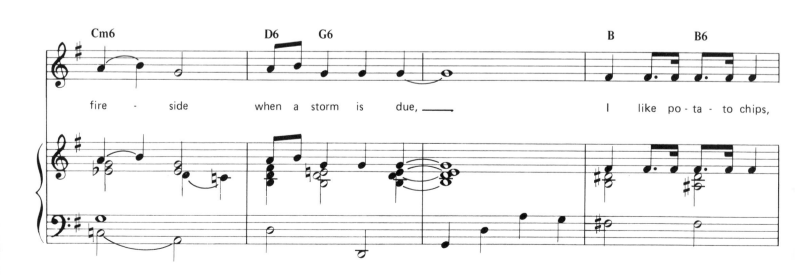

BABES ON BROADWAY

Lyric by RALPH FREED
Music By BURTON LANE

Martha Raye

Al Jolson

Jack Whiting

in

Bert Gordon

Hold On To Your Hats

Words by
E. Y. Harburg

Music by
Burton Lane

PRICE
60¢

Book by
Guy Bolton, Matty Brooks, Eddie Davis

Book Staged by
Edgar McGregor

Dances Staged by
Catherine Littlefield

Production Supervised by George Hale

Shubert Theatre
Opening Night September 11, 1940

(LOVE IS A LOVELY THING)
DON'T LET IT GET YOU DOWN

Words by E.Y. HARBURG
Music by BURTON LANE

Give it a swell fare-well,_____ What if it does-n't last for-

-ev - er___ Bet-ter a lit - tle now than nev - er, ___

Shout it a - round the town but DON'T LET IT GET YOU

1.
DOWN.

2.
DOWN.

THE WORLD IS IN MY ARMS

Words by E.Y. HARBURG
Music by BURTON LANE

THERE'S A GREAT DAY COMING MAÑANA

Words by E.Y. HARBURG
Music by BURTON LANE

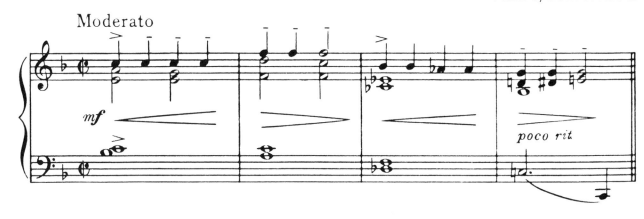

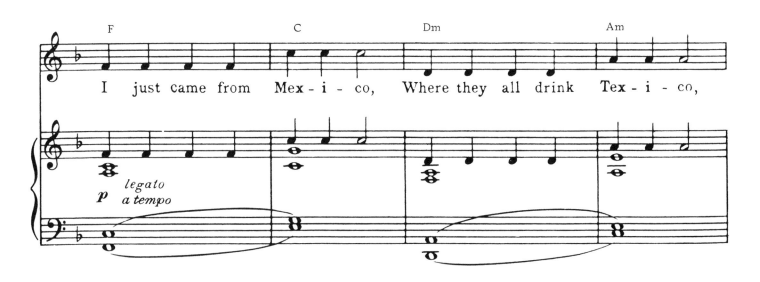

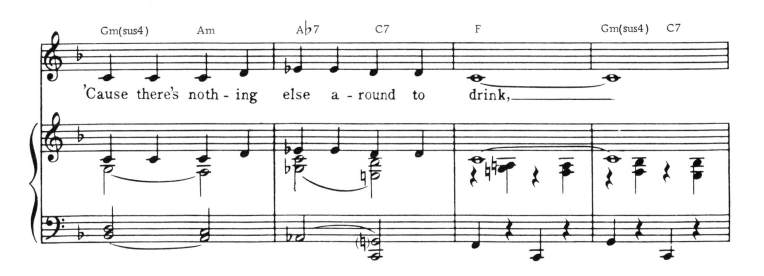

FEUDIN' AND FIGHTIN'

PRICE
60¢

LYRICS BY
AL DUBIN
AND
BURTON LANE
MUSIC BY
BURTON LANE

CHAPPELL
& CO. INC.

LAFFING ROOM ONLY
Winter Garden Theatre
Opening Night December 23, 1944

FEUDIN' AND FIGHTIN'

Words by AL DUBIN and BURTON LANE
Music by BURTON LANE

ROBERT FRYER and LAWRENCE CARR

with JOHN F. HERMAN

present

Finian's Rainbow

lyrics by **E. Y. HARBURG** · *music by* **BURTON LANE**

book by **E.Y. HARBURG & FRED SAIDY**

PRICE
60ᶜ

ALSO PUBLISHED FROM THE SCORE

Necessity	Look To The Rainbow
Old Devil Moon	The Begat
If This Isn't Love	When The Idle Poor
How Are Things in Glocca Morra	Become The Idle Rich
That Great Come-And-Get-It Day	Something Sort Of Grandish
When I'm Not Near The Girl I Love	Selection —

46th St. Theatre
Opening Night January 10, 1947

NECESSITY

Words by E.Y. HARBURG
Music by BURTON LANE

Recitative (very slowly)

What is the curse that makes the un-i-verse so all be-

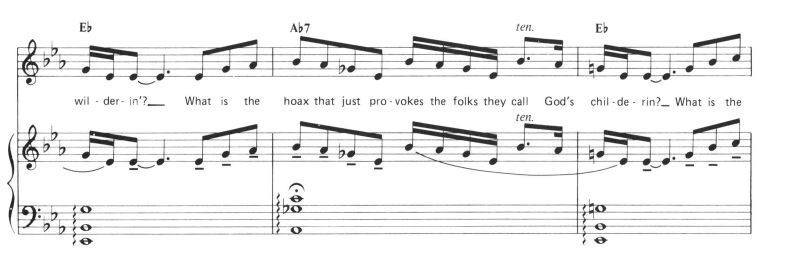

wil-der-in'?__ What is the hoax that just pro-vokes the folks they call God's chil-de-rin?__ What is the

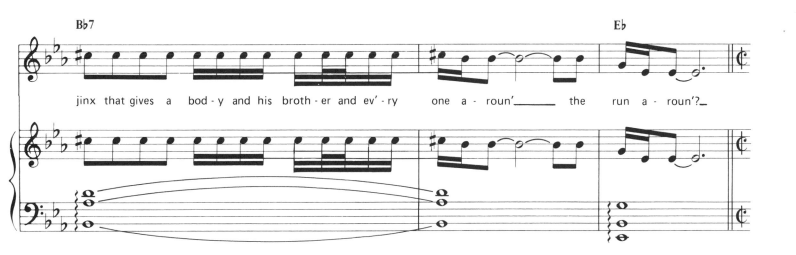

jinx that gives a bod-y and his broth-er and ev'-ry one a-roun'_____ the run a-roun'?__

HOW ARE THINGS IN GLOCCA MORRA

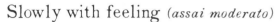

Words by E.Y. HARBURG
Music by BURTON LANE

Slowly with feeling (*assai moderato*)

IF THIS ISN'T LOVE
(From "Finian's Rainbow")

Words by E.Y. HARBURG
Music by BURTON LANE

OLD DEVIL MOON
(From "Finian's Rainbow")

Words by E.Y. HARBURG
Music by BURTON LANE

SOMETHING SORT OF GRANDISH

Words by E.Y. HARBURG
Music by BURTON LANE

86

Burton Lane

Burton Lane

Lyricist Harold Adamson and Burton Lane

Burton Lane (2nd from right) with Soviet composer Dmitri Kabalevsky (seated-2nd from right)

Burton Lane and Dorothy Fields

Al Jolson

HOLD ON TO YOUR HATS
with Al Jolson and Martha
Raye (1940)

OLUME 14   JUNE 30, 1940   NUMBER 30

The
PLAYGOER
TRADE MARK

A Magazine for the Theatre

FINIAN'S RAINBOW with David Wayne as the leprechaun Og (top photo)

Fred Astaire, Petula Clark, Tommy Steele in the film FINIAN's RAINBOW

Barbara Harris in Broadway's ON A CLEAR DAY YOU CAN SEE FOREVER

Barbra Streisand & Yves Montand in ON A CLEAR DAY - Film

Composer Lane with Barbara Harris and John Cullum during "Clear Day" rehearsal

BURTON
LANE

MARVIN
HAMLISCH

MARTIN
CHARNIN

SHELDON
HARNICK

ANDREW
LLOYD
WEBBER

ADOLF
GREEN

THAT GREAT COME AND GET IT DAY

Words and Music by
E.Y. HARBURG and BURTON LANE

THE BEGAT

Words by E.Y. HARBURG
Music by BURTON LANE

108

110

Film version: October 9, 1968

LOOK TO THE RAINBOW

Words by E.Y. HARBURG
Music by BURTON LANE

1. On the day I was born, said my fa- ther, said
2. ('Twas a) sump- tu- ous gift to be- queath to a
3. (So I) bund- led me heart and I roamed the world

he, I've an el- e- gant leg- a- cy
child, Oh the lure of that song kept her
free, To the east with the lark, to the

waitin' for ye, 'Tis a rhyme for your
feet runnin' wild. For you never your grow
west with the sea; And I searched all the

lips ____ and a song for your heart, ___ To
old ____ and you never stand still, ___ With
earth ____ and I scanned all the skies, ___ But I

sing it whenever the world falls apart.
whippoorwills singin' beyond the next hill.
found it at last in my own true love's eyes.

Refrain (*very slowly, with great expression*)

Look, look, Look to the Rainbow, Follow it

WHEN I'M NOT NEAR THE GIRL I LOVE

Words by E.Y. HARBURG
Music by BURTON LANE

Interlude

75¢

ON a CLEAR DaY You Can See Forever

A New Musical

Book and Lyrics by
ALAN JAY LERNER · BURTON LANE
Music by

Original Cast Album RCA Victor

Also published separately from the score: Hurry! It's Lovely Up Here! • What Did I Have That I Don't Have? • Come Back To Me • Melinda She Wasn't You • Wait Till We're Sixty-Five • On A Clear Day (You Can See Forever) • On The S. S. Bernard Cohn • When I'm Being Born Again

Mark Hellinger Theatre
Opening Night October 17, 1965
Film version: July 17, 1970

HURRY! IT'S LOVELY UP HERE!

Words by ALAN JAY LERNER
Music by BURTON LANE

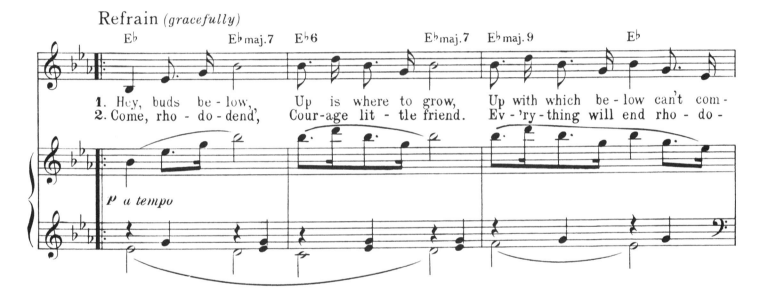

1. Hey, buds be - low, Up is where to grow, Up with which be - low can't com-
2. Come, rho - do - dend', Cour - age lit - tle friend. Ev - 'ry - thing will end rho - do -

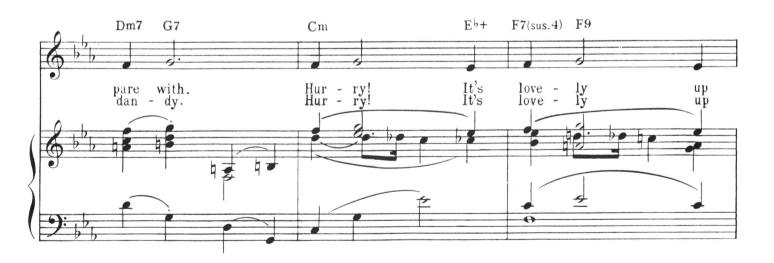

pare with.   Hur - ry!   It's   love - ly   up
dan - dy.   Hur - ry!   It's   love - ly   up

SHE WASN'T YOU

Words by ALAN JAY LERNER
Music by BURTON LANE

ON A CLEAR DAY
(YOU CAN SEE FOREVER)

Words by ALAN JAY LERNER
Music by BURTON LANE

WAIT TIL WE'RE SIXTY-FIVE

Words by ALAN JAY LERNER
Music by BURTON LANE

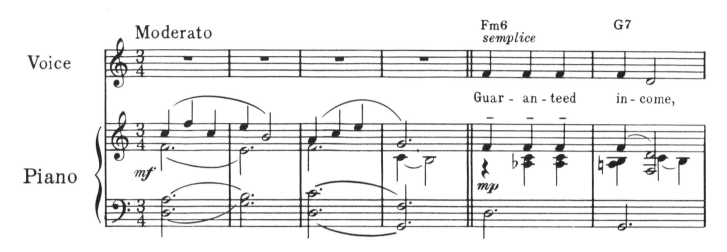

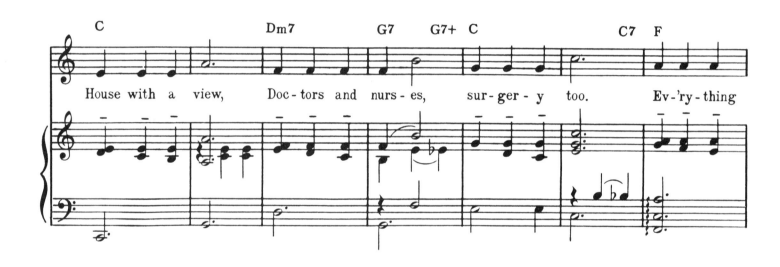

Refrain (*in strong rhythm and vigorously*)

ON THE S. S. BERNARD COHN

Words by ALAN JAY LERNER
Music by BURTON LANE

140

MELINDA

Words by ALAN JAY LERNER
Music by BURTON LANE

Slow waltz tempo

Refrain (*with feeling*)

This is a dream, Me- lin- da;____ Just a mir-

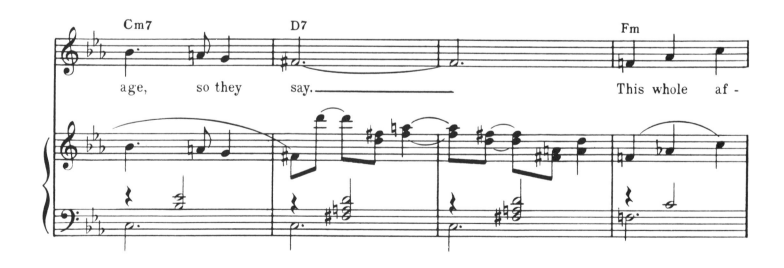

age, so they say.____ This whole af-

LOVE WITH ALL THE TRIMMINGS

Words by ALAN JAY LERNER
Music by BURTON LANE

WHAT DID I HAVE THAT I DON'T HAVE?

Words by ALAN JAY LERNER
Music by BURTON LANE

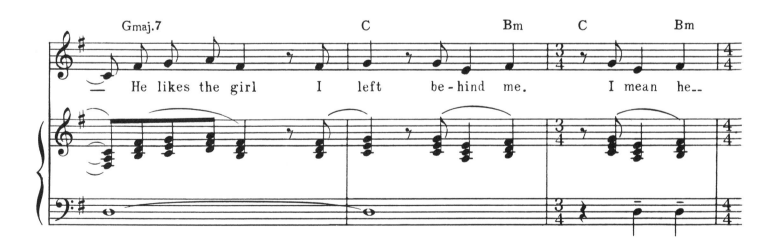

COME BACK TO ME

Words by ALAN JAY LERNER
Music by BURTON LANE

IT'S TIME FOR A LOVE SONG

Words by ALAN JAY LERNER
Music by BURTON LANE

WHERE HAVE I SEEN YOUR FACE BEFORE

Words by E.Y. HARBURG
Music By BURTON LANE

Where have I seen your face be-fore? Where have your eyes met

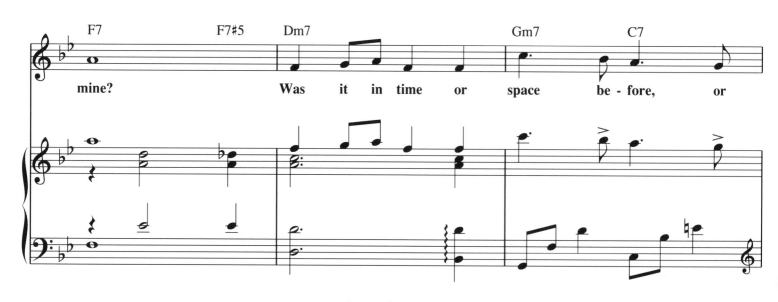

mine? Was it in time or space be-fore, or

ONE MORE WALK AROUND THE GARDEN

Words by ALAN JAY LERNER
Music by BURTON LANE

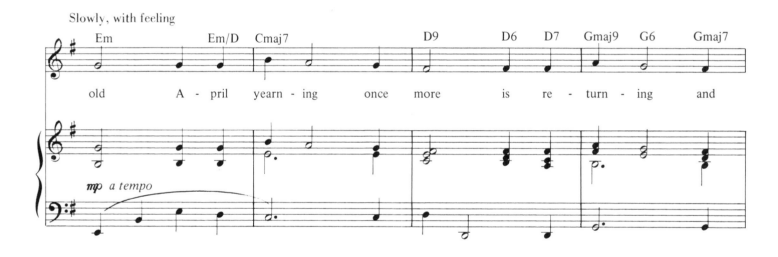

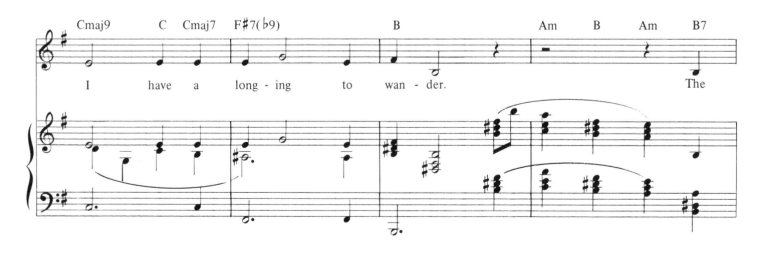